To Rich,

To You...

Sharon Madsen

MW00424030

All Rights Reserved

Copyright © 2017 by Sharon Madsen

This book may not be reproduced in whole or in part by any means without the permission of the Author.

Sharon Madsen
Foodsense A to Z "Helping you Make Sense of Food"

ISBN-10: 0692935649   USA
ISBN-13: 978-0692935644   EU

Madsen Publishing
Fountain Hills, AZ.

TYPE 2 DIABETES

"I contacted Sharon when my mom was diagnosed with Type 2 Diabetes at the age of 75. Sharon took the time to talk with my mom, understand her lifestyle, her likes and dislikes, and developed a plan to manage the disease that worked for her. That was over 5 years ago.

Today, thanks to Sharon's support and guidance, my mom still leads a very active life and is armed with great information to manage the condition to keep her blood sugar levels in check. Tom, California

FAMILY NUTRITION

"Between being a busy mom and co-owning a company, it can be difficult to juggle work, family, exercise, and eating healthy. Sharon makes it possible for me to feed my family healthy food that fuel our bodies and minds every single day.

I love coming home on Monday evenings after Sharon has prepared meals for the whole entire week. I don't know what I would do without her... she is a crucial part of our healthy lifestyle." Erin, Scottsdale

Table of Contents

Forward

I met Sharon Madsen at a high school baseball game standing next to a row of bleachers on a hot Arizona afternoon. Our sons were in different grades, but as baseball parents, we both screamed encouragement for the Saguaro Sabercats.

Fast forward through the next ten years. As a media designer, I have watched her business grow and her audience expand locally and across the country.
As with any small business, she has had to jump many hurdles in her journey as a single mom and non-stop entrepreneur.
In addition to her role as a personal nutrition consultant, her resume now includes public speaking, author, corporate nutritional partner, radio show host and promoter of local and regional organic farmers at local farmer's markets, chamber of commerce events and health fairs.

For those who have slipped into bad eating habits and even worse, health consequences, Sharon offers hope through better food choices.
For parents who want to keep their family healthy by eating real food, and staying out of the drive-through lane, this is where her expertise comes into place.

Lastly, for those interested in learning the truth about the food we eat, Sharon can help dispel the myths and replace them with nutritional language that everyone can understand and build into their lives.

Dan Watts
Entrepreneur, media designer, creative strategist and Dad.
www.nextworldmedia.com

Welcome to the simple way to make sense about food...Let's have some fun!

We hear a lot about changing our lives to a healthier lifestyle, but what does that actually mean? For some of us, it means making better choices with the foods we choose, getting more exercise and get proper rest.

Living this way maybe more of a challenge than you think.
Creating good habits takes time. It doesn't happen overnight.
Once you have a goal in mind, it's a lot easier to start changing the habits you've been raised with from childhood.

Emotions play a huge part in what we choose to eat.
We eat because we are happy, sad, upset, or excited.
We go out to dinner to celebrate the big promotion we have received at work or we may go out to dinner for love and support when bad news comes our way as well.

1

We all choose foods to match our emotions as things come up in our lives.   After choosing these foods to satisfy our emotions, we quickly realize that the choices we have made are not setting well with our bodies.

For most of us, in our busy lives, we have been known to "grab and go" when it comes to eating. The definition of this for most people would be headed through a "drive-through" to grab a burger, fries and soda.

Planning what you eat is an important part of eating healthy.

Having a well- stocked refrigerator with items that you can easily grab and go makes sense!

I'll assist you in figuring out what your refrigerator should have in it to fit the taste buds of your family members. If you shop and plan on the weekend you can have quick, simple and healthy meals on the table in minutes. All you need is one day to prepare for the week.

Which brings me to where I am today.
I want to help people eat better for their health and happiness.

That's a pretty tall order but I think if you follow along and take baby steps in the right direction you can be healthier and happier.

Stick with me and we will work together.

Refrigerator 101

The items in your refrigerator will become your best friend as the busy week unfolds.

The table below is a list of items to keep on hand.

All of these items can also be placed in a SALAD... you can have any combination you wish. (A Note on Salad dressings, read labels for low sodium and sugar content)

Shredded cheese	Raw sunflower seeds	Raw almonds
Hard boiled eggs	Shredded carrots	Raw pecans
Low sodium lunch meats	Butter lettuce	Raisins
Cooked chicken	Fresh Spinach	Corn tortillas
Cooked salmon	Oranges (quartered)	WW tortillas
Beans of any kind (drained)	Grapes	salsa
Squash	Grape Seed tomatoes	Green sauce
Ground beef, turkey, or chicken	Cucumbers (peeled or sliced)	Cooked Chicken (deboned or skinless)

Having these delicious foods prepared and in your refrigerator ready to go at a moments notice is important. As long as you have an ice chest, portable ice and a few containers to place foods in you are set! For storage in the refrigerator, use Zip Lock baggies or if you wish you can use containers.

Other foods to keep on hand would be
quinoa (cooked)
brown rice (cooked)
whole Wheat bread
whole wheat pita pockets

Keep in mind that having all of these things readily available to you makes it easier for you to "grab and go" to work, school activities and sporting events.
Making sure you are eating for fuel and nutrients is a better idea.
With the foods above you are less likely to stop and grab junk foods.

Having an idea of what your family likes to eat and plenty of items for them to choose from is important. Everyone will be happy and will tend to go to the refrigerator first when they want to eat or snack instead of walking to a cabinet full of goodies.

Water

Water is the most important drink to fuel your body. Headaches and lack of mental clarity is sometimes due to the fact that you are dehydrated. Keeping your body hydrated properly is very important! Here are some reasons why we need water...

Water is needed to break down and help foods to be digested.
Water carries nutrients from the food into the bloodstream to where they are needed and to eliminate any waste. Food cannot be digested without water.

Water helps digested food pass through the body quicker, preventing constipation and any toxins and waste material from sitting inside the body for too long and accumulating to dangerous levels.
Drinking water helps to;

1. Regulate the temperature of the body and body heat.

2. Keeps the kidneys healthy and in working order and prevents urinary infections from occurring.

3. Keep joints and eyes lubricated, and acts as a protective cushion for tissues and cells.

4. Keeps skin looking younger and well-hydrated.

5. Aids in keeping skin supple and looking healthy and glowing.

6. Water is the main component of muscles and keeps them toned and firm. Lack of water will result in cramping of muscles.

7. Increase blood circulation.

8. Dilute toxins and removes them from the body (When we remove toxins we are less likely to carry diseases around with us.

9. Aids in circulation.

10. Aids in the metabolism and elimination of fats. Without water, fat deposits in the body will increase.

11. Drinking water will alleviate water retention and lessen swelling of hands and feet.

The brain is comprised of a lot of water and therefore needs replenishment to keep it working well and to full capacity. Without water we may lose concentration and suffer headaches and tiredness.

Water dilutes the calcium in our urine, which could crystallize to form kidney stones if the body did not receive enough fluids.

Fruits, Vegetables, & Color

Eating 9 to 13 servings per day of fruits and vegetables is best. I know this seems like a lot but if you pace yourself and look at portions, you will probably see that it can be more realistic than you imagine.

One serving is the size of your palm. So when you snack and grab a handful of grapes and a handful of berries this would equal 2 serving sizes.

These items are way better choices than sitting down to watch TV and eating $\frac{3}{4}$ of a bag of Lays potato chips.

The Power of Red...Lycopene is great for the heart and great for fighting cancers.

The Power of Green...best source of calcium, lutein's fight against prostate cancer,

The Power of Orange/Yellow... beta carotenes, eyesight, cancer, Vitamin. C resource.

The Power of White... (garlic, scallions) keeps sickness away, immune booster.

The Power of Purple/Blue... flavonoids, antioxidants, anthocyanin's body's defense of harmful carcinogens, Vitamin C resource, folic acid, potassium.

Try adding a variety of fruits and vegetables to your family's diet.

You would be surprised to find many recipes or preparation ideas for the new foods you are willing to try.
Just because you are not familiar with a product, don't let that stop you from doing a little research to figure out how to try it... I challenge each of you to take 5 minutes each week and try a new food with a new preparation.
It could be fun...

The Power of Red...

Lycopene is great for the heart and great for fighting cancers.

- A healthy heart
- Memory function
- A lower risk of some cancers

- Urinary tract health

Beets	Radishes	Tomatoes
Red Bell Peppers	Red Potatoes	Red Grapefruit
Watermelon	Strawberries	Raspberries
Cranberries	Blood Oranges	Cherries
Pomegranates		

It's no wonder that the color of these fruits and vegetables are the same color as our blood.

Blood contains a protein called hemoglobin. Hemoglobin, which contains iron, is found in red blood cells and is the ingredient that makes blood red.

Blood is an important **fluid** that keeps us alive.

The heart pumps blood to all parts of the body and brings them **oxygen** and food.

At the same time blood carries away all the substances that we don't need.

Eating several RED fruits and vegetables each day will ensure the healthiest blood.

The Power of Green...

best source of calcium, luteins, fight against prostate cancer.

- A lower risk of some cancers
- Vision health
- Strong bones and teeth

Green apples	Green pears	Kiwi fruit
Green grape	Honeydew	Limes

Artichokes	Cabbage	Fennel	Leafy Greens
Arugula	Celery	Green Beans	Lettuce
Asparagus	Chard	Green Olives	Okra
Avocados	Cilantro	Green Onion	Parsley
Basil	Cucumbers	Green Peppers	Snow peas
Bok Choy	Edamame	Jalapeno	Spinach
Broccoli	Endive	Kale	Sugar snap peas
Brussel Sprouts			Zucchini

The Power of Orange/Yellow

Beta carotenes, and a Vitimin C resource.

- A healthy heart
- Vision health
- A healthy immune system
- A lower risk of some cancers

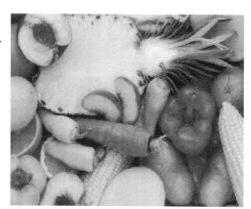

Carrots	Corn	Sweet Potatoes
Cantaloupe	Yellow Peppers	Yams
Pumpkin	Yellow Squash	Apricots
Oranges	Peaches	

Yellow and Orange fruits and vegetables are full of antioxidants, vitamins and fiber.

These colorful foods assist in eliminating toxins, improve skin condition, improve eye and heart health, boost the immune system and help break down fatty foods in the digestive system.

The Power of White...

Immune boosters,
keeps sickness
away
Better Heart
Health
Lowers Cholesterol
levels
Lowers risk of
some cancers

White fruits and vegetables act as natural antibiotics and cancer inhibitors. They also help to lower blood pressure by reducing fat deposits in the arteries. They contain high concentrations of potassium, fiber and promote healthy skin.

Brown pears	Cauliflower Garlic	Jerusalem Artichoke	Potatoes (white Fleshed)
Dates	Ginger	Kohlraabi	Shallots
White Nectarines	Ginger	Mushrooms & Onions	Turnips
White Peaches	Jicama	Parsnips	White corn

The Power of Purple/Blue...

Flavonoids, antioxidants, Anthocyanins body's defense
of harmful carcinogens,
Vitamin C resource, folic acid, potassium.

- lowers risk of some cancers
- Urinary tract
  health
- Memory function
- Healthy aging

Blackberries	Elderberries	Raisins	Eggplant
Blueberries	Purple Figs	Purple Asparagus	Purple Belgian endive
Blackcurrants	Purple Grapes	Purple Cabbage	Purple Peppers
Dried Plums	Plums	Purple Carrots	Potatoes (Purple Fleshed)

A Few Words About The Digestive System

The digestive system breaks down all of the food you eat which is later transported throughout the body by the circulatory system.

A healthy digestive system requires:
- balanced diet of protein, fat, carbohydrate, vitamins, minerals, fiber, and water.
- Regular physical activity.
- Stress management.

Diets low in saturated fat and cholesterol and high in fiber decrease the risk of:
- certain cancers, such as colon cancer
- diabetes
- digestive disorders
- heart disease

Fiber

There are certain nutrients and substances that affect digestion: **Soluble fiber** dissolves in the digestive system completely.

There are two types of soluble fiber: pectin and gum. Pectin, found in apples and oranges, helps other nutrients to digest.

Gum, found in many fruits, vegetables, and oats, positively affects the absorption of cholesterol and glucose in the bloodstream.

Insoluble fiber adds bulk to the GI tract and helps move waste out. Examples are: cellulose, hemicellulose, and lignin.   B-complex helps maintain a healthy GI tract.

Enzymes such as lipase, cellulase, and bromelain, aid in the digestion and assimilation of protein, fat, carbohydrate, and fiber.
Herbs such as goldenrod, black spruce, poison nut, and wild hops, help calm and soothe an upset or acidic stomach.

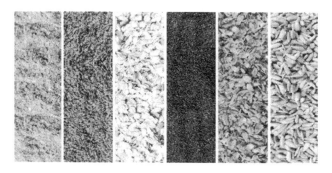

Five foods that boost your mood!

Bananas

Bananas offer serious mood-lifting power
with their combination of
vitamins
B6, A and C; fiber,
tryptophan, potassium,
phosphorous, iron, protein,
and healthy
carbohydrates.

When you eat a banana,
you'll get a quick
boost from the fructose as well as sustaining
energy from the fiber, which helps prevent a
blood sugar spike and ensuing drop in energy and mood.

Carbohydrates aid in the absorption of tryptophan in
the brain, and vitamin B6 helps convert the tryptophan
into mood-lifting serotonin.

Bananas are also a great source of potassium. While potassium isn't directly related to mood, it's needed to regulate fluid levels and keep muscles working properly, which is important for feeling energized, a key factor for being an "energizer bunny". LOL.

Bananas also offer iron, which is crucial to producing energy and fighting fatigue.

Get creative with bananas. Top your cooked oatmeal, quinoa, breakfast cereal with slices of bananas. Mash them up and add to recipes of scones, breads, pancakes and waffles. Peel and eat bananas dunking them in nut butters of your choice. keep them around for an easy, "quick pick me" up snack.

Best of all, bananas are available year-round and are easy to carry -- just make sure to pack them on top of your lunch box, they bruise easily.

Walnuts

Walnuts contain a handful of components that contribute to a good mood, including omega-3s, vitamin B6, tryptophan, protein, and folate.

Higher blood levels of omega-3s have been linked with better mood and lower rates of depression, while lower blood levels of omega-3s have been associated with higher rates of depression and negative feelings.

It's been said that walnuts have omega-3s and uridine (a substance found in walnuts, which plays an important role in helping metabolize carbohydrates) which is believed to be an antidepressant.

The standard dosage of omega-3 oils recommended by many experts is one gram (1,000 mg) per day. You'll get about the same amount, as well as a healthy dose of fiber and protein, in just half an ounce of walnuts.

Who would ever have thought that walnuts could be a "feel good nut"?

Get creative with walnuts. chopped walnuts can be added to oatmeal, homemade granola, muffins, used instead of pine nuts in a pesto sauce, savory dishes such as poultry, and pork. Eaten by the handful, these brown pieces of goodness can really make a difference in the way you feel.

Sunflower Seeds

Sunflower seeds are a
super source of folate
and magnesium, two
substances that play a
significant role in
regulating and boosting
mood.

Just a handful of sunflower seeds deliver half
the daily recommended amount for magnesium.
Magnesium, in addition to regulating mood, plays an
essential role in hundreds of bodily functions.
Magnesium deficiency is often responsible for feelings
of fatigue, nervousness, and anxiety (since it triggers
an increase in adrenaline), and it's been linked to
various mood disorders.
Sufficient, stable magnesium levels, on the other hand,
help us achieve a calm and relaxed state. We all want
to be more relaxed, right?

It's so effective, in fact, that some studies have shown
magnesium supplementation to be beneficial in treating
major depression, suicidal tendencies, anxiety,
irritability, and insomnia.

Folate (also known as vitamin B9 and as folic acid) is a B-complex vitamin that's intimately linked with nervous system function. Folate deficiency may result in feelings of irritability, depression, and brain fog, as well as insomnia. Who wants to sleep better at night? Add sunflower seeds for better sleep!

Being well rested and keeping a clear head are two of the primary factors in fueling a good mood, so snacking on sunflower seeds is a smart move in more ways than one. If you are trying to function in a fog, you'll lose this battle.

Sunflower seeds are a good source of tryptophan and are often recommended by nutritional experts as a natural method of boosting serotonin levels.
They're also rich in fiber, which helps maintain stable hormone levels -- one of the keys to keeping even-keeled.

Get creative with sunflower seeds.

Whether you eat them by the handful or in a salad, sunflower seeds are small enough to place in a baggie and carry with you for a quick crunchy snack.

Eggs

Eggs might not be the first food that comes
to mind when you think of a snack, but a
hard-boiled egg is easy
to make and easy to
transport.

It's also a really good-
for-you and good-for-
your-mood snack.

Full of high-quality protein and omega-3s
(from hens eating a diet rich in omega-3s), eggs are also
an excellent source of vitamin B12 (riboflavin) and a
good source of vitamins B2, B5, and D.

One boiled egg contains more than 20 percent of the
daily recommended amount of tryptophan.

While carbs are crucial for converting tryptophan into
serotonin, protein is an important part of the process,
too. A balanced diet that includes high-quality lean
protein, like you find in eggs, and healthy carbs also
helps stabilize blood sugar and prevent emotional highs
and lows.

The Vitamin B12 in eggs plays a significant role in the production of energy and helps alleviate many problems and symptoms of depression.
Protein is your best source of "get up and go" energy.
It is the fuel that you need to start your day.

Get creative with eggs.
Hard boiled eggs are the staple in our home.
We always have them for a quick snack or energy boost.
Topping a salad with hard boiled eggs is a great way to help create a protein and vegetable rich meal.

Dark Chocolate

Who doesn't like chocolate?
I love dark chocolate! Did you know that chocolate is the
number-one craved food in America?
WOW!
Here are some
reasons why that
is true.
Chocolate contains
a number of
substances that
elevate mood,

including fat, sugar, caffeine,
phenyl ethylamine, flavonols, Theobromine and
tryptophan.
Caffeine and Theobromine are two naturally occurring
stimulants found in chocolate. Along with sugar and fat,
these substances provide a swift burst of energy and
mood-lifting power. Chocolate also contains the mood-
boosting compounds phenyl ethylamine, tyramine,
tryptophan, and magnesium.
While these substances are found in many other foods,
even in higher concentrations, chocolate has an
advantage because of its appeal on several sensory

levels. It has a rich, mouth-pleasing texture; an intense taste; and smells awesome! For many of us, just the idea of indulging in chocolate is enough to trigger a positive emotional response. YUMMY!

It makes sense that indulging in chocolate makes for a happy and satisfying experience. In addition to these natural pick-me-ups, when you eat chocolate, a number of reactions occur, including the release of serotonin in the brain and mood elevating endorphins in the body. This combination can result in a temporarily lifted mood and feeling euphoria, which may explain why some people turn to chocolate when they're feeling blue.

Finally, cocoa is a natural source of antioxidant flavonoids which increase blood flow in the brain, and which may contribute to better brain function.

Not all chocolate is created equal.
For the best health and happiness benefits look for good-quality dark chocolate with a cocoa level of 70 percent or higher. The more cocoa chocolate contains, the higher the levels of healthy compounds. The darker the chocolate, the better it is for you.

Chocolate in moderation is GOOD for you.
Imagine that!!

6 Foods That Keep You Cool In The Summer

In the wintertime we tend to eat more cooked food. Why? Cooked food is hot food and warms the body.

If it's cold outside you aren't going to reach for watermelon when you walk in your door.

The idea of eating seasonally works well for many people. You eat seasonally to benefit from the seasonal growing. At the same time this idea applies to cooked and raw food. In the wintertime eating a hot soup or cooked potatoes keeps your body warm and metabolism moving right along when it needs to be. The same applies in the summertime. The foods that keep you cool also give you plenty of energy on the hot summer days.

1. Cucumber: If you want to cool down in the summertime then grab a cucumber and cut some slices up. There's a reason people say you're cool as a cucumber all the time, it's one of the most cooling foods.

The water content in cucumber is higher than most foods on the planet so you're hydrating and cooling your body at the same time.

2. Watermelon:

Watermelon is also one of the most hydrating water dense foods on the planet. Because of this it's inherently cooling to your body. Think of watermelon as an internal air conditioning unit, just keep it on and keep eating! This addictive summertime fruit also contains lycopene which is an antioxidant that prevents sunburn and UV ray damage. It's made for summer consumption.

3. Peaches:

Peaches are a cooling and enriching summertime treat. They're naturally hydrating to the body and contain nutrients that benefit your health in many other ways.

4. Apples:

Let's get crispy! Apples offer that cool, refreshing, crisp crunch that make summers a bit easier and more bearable. They're always a cooling bite away.

5. Pineapple:

Pineapple is another water rich fruit that is cooling and refreshing to the body. This is a great fruit to add to a smoothie. Take a bit of pineapple, banana, kale and cucumber and you've got yourself a superfood nutrient dense cooling smoothie.

6. Lemon:

Lemon is a rich source of vitamin c and gives you a refreshing cool kick of energy as well. Foods that cool your body and give your body energy do more as the heat wears your body down. Squeeze an organic lemon into a glass of water and enjoy

Ten Foods to help you sleep through the night

Getting a good night sleep is a difficult task for many adults. Some people have a hard time falling asleep, some have a hard time staying asleep and some people have a hard time finding the time to sleep. Regardless of which category you fall into, getting a good amount of quality shut-eye each night is critical in maintaining your overall health.

A good night sleep will not only provide you with more energy the next day but it will keep your immune system strong, your skin radiant and your blood pressure low – all key components to great health.

If you're looking for ways to get a good night sleep, you might want to start with your diet. Eating the following foods will help you sleep like a baby – and wake up feeling refreshed and ready to start your day.

Here are 10 foods to help you sleep through the night.

1. Fish

Most types of fish are jam-packed with Vitamin B6. This vitamin is needed to make melatonin – a sleep-promoting hormone which is triggered by darkness. If you're going to add fish to your diet, salmon, tuna and halibut boast the highest levels of Vitamin B6.

2. Chickpeas

Much like fish, chickpeas are packed full of Vitamin B6 which is needed to make melatonin. Chickpeas can be eaten on their own or crushed and mixed with other ingredients to make a healthy hummus dip. A few spoonfuls of this tasty snack will have you sleeping better in no time.

3. Bananas

Bananas are rich in both potassium and Vitamin B6. Combined these nutrients are very effective in promoting a good night sleep and keeping you healthy overall. Eating a banana before bed will help you achieve a better night sleep.

4. Yogurt

Research has linked difficulty falling asleep to a lack of calcium. Eating foods rich in calcium can reverse these effects and help you fall asleep faster. A bowl of yogurt in the evening will give you a boost of calcium which will help you get better quality shut-eye.

5. Tart Cherry Juice

A recent study showed that individuals with chronic insomnia who drank two glasses of tart cherry juice a day immediately experienced some relief in their symptoms. This well-known sleep aid will put you to sleep in no time.

6. Whole Grains

If you're experiencing difficulty sleeping it may be because your magnesium levels are too low. Whole grains, like barley, couscous and buckwheat, offer high levels of magnesium which will not only help you fall asleep but will help you stay asleep longer.

7. Fortified Cereals

Much like fish and chickpeas, fortified cereals are a great source of Vitamin B6. As noted earlier, Vitamin B6 is essential in producing melatonin (a sleep inducing hormone). If you're looking for a good night sleep, down a bowl of fortified cereal (like Wheaties, Frosted Flakes or multi-grain Cheerios) before bed and start sleeping like a baby every night.

8. Almonds

Almonds, like whole grains, have high levels of magnesium, which is essential for good sleep. "Almonds are a winner," Jacob Teitelbaum, MD, medical director of the Fibromyalgia and Fatigue Centers, and author of the bestselling book FROM FATIGUED TO FANTASTIC! "They contain magnesium, which promotes both sleep and muscle relaxation." A handful of these before bed will put you right to sleep.

9. Decaf Tea

Everyone knows that caffeine will keep you awake, but there are countless decaf teas that are proven to help you sleep. "Chamomile tea is a very helpful and safe sleep aid," Dr. Teitelbaum says, adding that green tea is another good choice. "Green tea contains theanine, which helps promote sleep. Just be sure you get a decaf green tea if drinking it at bed time. A cup of tea at night will help you get the quality shut-eye you've been looking for.

10. Hard Boiled Eggs

Eating a snack with high levels of protein before bed will help you stay asleep through the night. If you wake up several times throughout the night, it could be because your body isn't getting enough protein. Eating a hard-boiled egg before bed will not only help you fall asleep but will help you stay asleep right and into the morning.

Smoothies

Digestive Smoothie Recipe

Bananas and apples contain pectin, which helps remove toxins and excess cholesterol from the digestive tract. It also encourages the growth of beneficial bacteria in the gut, which is essential to maintain harmony and prevent the overgrowth of bad bacteria such as Candida Albicans.

Pumpkin Seeds are excellent for prostate health. They help remove intestinal parasites. Pumpkin seed oil is rich in omega-3 essential fatty acids (but do not heat or the value is destroyed). They are also rich in Calcium, Iron, Magnesium, Zinc, B vitamins, Phosphorus, Potassium and Omega-3 essential fatty acids.

Apples are an astringent tonic. They Relieve constipation, reactivate beneficial gut bacteria and reduce total cholesterol. They also help remove toxins and are rich in Calcium, Magnesium, Phosphorus, Vitamin C, Beta-carotene and Pectin

Tofu has phyto-estrogenic properties that regulate any excess circulating estrogens, which may play a part in the buildup of arterial plaque.

Bananas help you sleep well. They are a mild laxative, anti-fungal and a natural antibiotic.

Bananas also contain pectin which helps ulcers, lowers cholesterol and removes toxic metals from the body. They are rich in Potassium, Tryptophan, Vitamin C, Beta-carotene, Vitamin K and Vitamin B6

Ingredients ... You will need
- 3 teaspoons of pumpkin seeds
- 14 oz. of organic tofu
- 2 bananas
- 2 medium unpeeled apples
- 6 cups of almond milk

-Quarter and core the apples but do not peel them
-Drain and cube the tofu
-Grind the pumpkin seeds in a food processor or coffee grinder to release their essential -fats and prevent any irritation in the gut.
-Add the remainder of the smoothie ingredients and then blend for 1-2 minutes until smooth.

Enjoy!

Green Goodness Smoothie
(full of anti-oxidants)

1 cup Spinach
1 cup cucumber chunks
$\frac{1}{2}$ avocado chopped
1 large Kiwi peeled and chopped
$\frac{1}{2}$ cup almond milk
$\frac{1}{2}$ cup orange juice
chopped mint leaves

Blend all in a blender till smooth. Add ice if desired
ENJOY!

Liver Cleansing Smoothie

1 cup of chopped zucchini
1 clove garlic
1 cup of cabbage
2 cups of celery
1 cup of kale
1 cup of ice
3 carrots to add sweetness.
Blend all ingredients
Your liver will thank you!

Lymphatic Smoothie

1 large banana
1 cup of strawberries
1/2 cup of fresh orange juice,
1 cup of pineapple
1 cup of ice

Blend all ingredients

Turmeric and Ginger Smoothie
aids in digestion and inflammation

1 ripe banana
2 teaspoons Almond butter
1/2 teaspoon turmeric powder
1 teaspoon fresh grated ginger
1/2 cup Almond Milk
1 teaspoon flax oil
A few ice cubes

Add all ingredients to a blender and blend till smooth.

ENJOY!

Cucumber smoothie

2 servings

2 cups spinach
1 cup peeled and sliced cucumbers
1 cup honeydew melon
1 tablespoon lime juice
2 tablespoons chia seeds
Blend all

Tropical smoothie

2 cups spinach
2 cups chopped watermelon
1 cup peeled and sliced peaches
1 cup strawberries
Blend all
Enjoy!

Appetizers

Artichoke Hummus (makes 8 servings)

Not many people like the taste or consistency of artichokes. If you are one of these people, you have to try this. The creaminess of this hummus is awesome!

1 cup canned artichoke hearts, drained
1/4 cup fat-free vegetable broth 1/4 cup fat-free plain Greek yogurt
1 tbsp. lemon juice
2 tsps. crushed garlic
1/2 tsp. dried parsley flakes
1/4 tsp. ground cumin
1/4 tsp. smoked paprika
15-oz. can garbanzo beans, drained and rinsed

Directions:
Put all ingredients except garbanzo beans in a blender. Using a potato masher or a fork, thoroughly mash the garbanzo beans in a bowl. Transfer to the blender. Puree until smooth, stopping and stirring if blending slows.For best flavor, cover and refrigerate hummus for several hours. Serve with pita chips, cut veggies, or put a little bit of rice cakes.

Beet Hummus

Great for a party! Have a big plate of vegetables ready to dip into this bright red spread. Your guests will never know they are eating beets unless you decide to give the secret away!

½ pound beets (about 4 medium sized beets), scrubbed clean, cooked, peeled, and cubed
2 tbsp. sesame seed
5 tbsp. lemon juice
2 cloves garlic, minced
1 tbsp. ground cumin
1 tbsp. lemon zest (zest from approx. 2 lemons)
1 generous pinch of sea salt or Kosher salt
1 fresh ground pepper to taste

Boil Method
To cook the beets, cut off any tops, scrub the roots clean and cook until easily penetrated with a knife or fork.
Cover with water in a saucepan and simmer until tender, about 1/2 hour. Peel once they have cooled.

Roasting Method

Roasting beets intensifies their flavor, brings out their earthy sweetness.

Rinse any dirt or debris from the beets. Put beets on a large piece of aluminum foil covered cookie sheet and preheat the oven

to 375. Drizzle the beets with a bit of olive oil before roasting. The amount of time this will take can vary greatly depending on the size of the beets. For smaller beets, start checking them for tenderness at about 25 minutes. Larger and older beets can take up to an hour.

Remove beets from oven when tender. Let sit until cool enough to handle. When beets are cool enough to handle, slip their peels off. You can use a paring knife, if you like, but you can rub the beets with your fingers and the peels will come off easily.

Now, place all ingredients in a food processor (or blender) and pulse until smooth. Taste and adjust seasonings and ingredients as desired.

Chill and store in the refrigerator for up to 3 days. Eat with pita chips, sliced cucumber or maybe even celery

Cheesy Quinoa Bites

The quantity of these will vary depending on how big or small you decide to make them. These are delicious as a side dish or even keep some in your refrigerator as a snack!

2 cups cooked quinoa
2 large eggs, lightly beaten
1 medium carrot, shredded
2 tablespoons finely chopped pine nuts
2 scallions, finely chopped
3 cloves garlic, minced
1/4 cup chopped fresh parsley
1/2 cup grated Parmesan cheese (or any other mixture of cheeses you might like)
2 tablespoons gluten free flour
1/4 tsp. freshly ground pepper

-Preheat oven to 350 F. Lightly spray a mini muffin pan with nonstick cooking spray.

-Stir all of the ingredients in a medium bowl until well combined.

Use a small cookie scoop or tablespoon to divide the mixture evenly among the wells of the pan, you can fill them all the way to the top.

Lightly press down to make sure each well is packed. -Bake for 18-20 minutes, or until the bites are golden and set. Remove from the wells and serve.

ENJOY!

Cheesy Tortilla w/Black Bean Puree

This black bean puree can keep for up to 3 days in the refrigerator. It has many uses. This yummy puree can be used as a dip for pita chips, veggies, added to scrambled eggs, or even can be spooned into a baked potato and topped with a little shredded cheese.

4 cups of puree
4 cups cooked black beans
1 cup of fresh water
1 teaspoon garlic, minced
Pinch or sea salt and pepper
12 corn tortillas
1 $\frac{1}{2}$ cup Monterey Jack cheese

Toppings:
Avocado slices, Diced tomatoes
Green onions, sliced Olives or whatever you want to add!

 In a food processor blend black beans, garlic, sea salt, pepper and water. Blend till smooth but not runny. Transfer to a small pot and warm on simmer. Warm corn tortillas on a per person basis and start to fill with black bean puree and toppings.

HONEY CHIPOTLE TURKEY MEATBALLS (Serves 8)

The chipotle flavor really comes through in this recipe and the honey really boosts up the flavor as well. You can make a double batch of these as they freeze really well.

Preheat Oven to 375 degrees

1 1/2 pounds of Ground Turkey
1/2 yellow onion, chopped fine
2 cloves of garlic, minced
1/4 teaspoon each salt and pepper

Combine these ingredients till mixed (do not over mix) Form into meatballs. Add Extra Virgin Olive Oil to a skillet and brown meat on all sides and set meatballs aside. Approximately 10 minutes.

In a small bowl combine the following...
2 tablespoons Honey
2 tablespoons chopped chipotle chilies in Adobo sauce
 2 teaspoons apple cider vinegar.
1/4 teaspoon lemon zest
1/8 teaspoon smoked paprika

-On a greased Pyrex baking dish, spread out Turkey meatballs and coat with the sauce mixture using a baking brush.
-Bake until the liquid is reduced and the meatballs are glazed.

ENJOY!

Salads

Chicken, Green Beans and Apple Salad (Serves 4)

This crisp and clean salad can be made in advance and kept in the refrigerator for up to 3 days. I think that the jicama really makes this salad.

2 boneless, skinless chicken breasts, cooked
$\frac{1}{4}$ cup mayonnaise
2 tablespoons Red Wine Vinegar
2 tablespoons fresh tarragon leaves, chopped
1 tablespoon agave syrup
$\frac{1}{4}$ teaspoon sea salt
8 ounces fresh green beans, blanched
$\frac{1}{2}$ medium jicama, sliced thin
1 medium granny smith apple, sliced thin
$\frac{1}{4}$ cup golden raisins
3 cups mixed greens salad blend

Dressing... mayonnaise, red wine vinegar, agave syrup, sea salt and tarragon leaves. Mix well and let place in refrigerator for flavors to marry.

-Use 4 plates and divide up greens, chicken, jicama, apple, and raisins.

-Stir up dressing real well and drizzle over the 4 plates of delicious salad ingredients.

-Top with shredded cheese or Parmesan cheese if desired.

ENJOY!

Chicken Waldorf salad with Yogurt Dressing

Makes 2 cups of salad

I came up with this recipe for my friend. She wanted a recipe to be able to make in advance and take to work.

Ingredients:
1/4 cup plain yogurt (low fat)
1 cup cooked chicken, cut into small chunks
1 tablespoon fresh lemon juice
1/4 teaspoon sea salt
1/4 teaspoon pepper
1 medium apple, cored, cut into small chunks
1 stalk celery, chopped
1/2 cup red seedless grapes, cut in half
1/2 cup walnuts, chopped

Preparation:
Toss all ingredients into a bowl and refrigerate to let flavors marry.

There are so many variations on what you can do with this yummy salad. Here are a few ideas...

Salad can be placed on a Rice Cake along with lettuce, or in a pita pocket, or make a whole wheat sandwich.

You can also eat it by itself with crackers or make lettuce wraps with this awesome salad.

ENJOY!

Three Bean Pasta Salad

Serves 8

This is a great dish to make when you want a light dinner or maybe even an on-the-go lunch choice!!

6 ounces small pasta shells cooked AL Dente
3/4 lb. fresh green beans, trimmed and cut
2 tablespoons Dijon mustard
1/3 cup red wine vinegar or tarragon vinegar
2 tablespoons agave syrup
1/2 cup EVOO
1 can (15.5 ounces) white beans rinsed and drained
1 can (15.5 ounces) Garbanzo beans rinsed and drained
5 tablespoons of chopped red onion
3 celery stalks, sliced thin

-When cutting up vegetables make them all about the same size.
-In a medium bowl, combine all liquid ingredients first. mix well.
-Add remaining ingredients. You might want to add a bit of sea salt and pepper to taste... -Not too much, you'll want to taste the flavors of the oils and vinegar. This is an awesome quick dish

-You might want to add a bit of protein to this salad. Tuna, cooked salmon, or cut up chicken. Refrigerate for up to 2 days only.

ENJOY!

Tomato and cucumber salad

2 cucumbers, peeled and sliced, cut into chunks

2 tomatoes, cut into chunks

1 small red onion, cut into chunks

1 quarter cup finely grated Parmesan cheese

$\frac{1}{4}$ cup extra virgin olive oil

$\frac{1}{4}$ cup balsamic vinegar

1 tablespoon dried Italian seasoning

3 cloves garlic, minced

1 teaspoon basil

1 teaspoon sea salt

$\frac{1}{2}$ teaspoon black pepper

In a bowl place the prepared vegetables, cucumbers
Tomatoes, red onion. Sprinkle the grated Parmesan
cheese on top.

In a shaker bottle, combine extra-virgin olive oil, balsamic vinegar, Italian seasoning, garlic, basil, sea salt black pepper, and shake up well.

Pour over the vegetables and let marinade in the refrigerator for 1 hour to blend flavors and get cold.

Enjoy!

Agave Lime Fruit Salad

1-pound fresh strawberries, diced
1-pound fresh pineapple, diced
12 oz. fresh blueberries
12 oz. red grapes, halved
4 kiwis, peeled and diced
1 (15 ounce) can mandarin oranges in juice, drained well
and sliced into halves
2 ripe bananas, diced*

Agave Lime Dressing

1/4 cup agave syrup, organic
2 tsp lime zest (zest of 2 medium limes)
1 Tablespoon fresh lime juice

Add all fruit to a large mixing bowl.
In a small mixing bowl, whisk together the agave syrup,
lime zest and lime juice.
Pour over fruit just before serving and toss
to evenly coat.
Let this set up in the refrigerator and
stir again before serving to blend flavors

*The bananas are added just before serving

On The Side

Here are a few side dishes that are easy to prepare and delicious as well... You can double these recipes if you are feeding more people.

Shredded Carrots

2 tablespoons EVOO   (Extra Virgin Olive Oil)
2 tablespoons diced onions
1/4 teaspoon fennel seed
1/8 teaspoon paprika
1/4 teaspoon cumin
4 cups grated carrots
2 tablespoons lime juice

Sauté in EVOO, onions, fennel, paprika and cumin till fragrant in a medium bowl toss together the carrots and onion mixture. Add sea salt and pepper to taste.

Spicy Sautéed Celery

1 tablespoon butter
3 cloves garlic, sliced thin
1 large bunch of celery sliced thin
1/4 teaspoon red peppers.

In a large skillet, melt butter, add garlic and celery. Sauté till tender crisp about 6 minutes. season with red pepper flakes and sea salt.

Quinoa and Black Beans

1 teaspoon extra virgin olive oil

1 small yellow onion, chopped

3 cloves garlic, minced

$\frac{3}{4}$ cup quinoa

1 $\frac{1}{2}$ cups vegetable broth

1 teaspoon ground cumin

$\frac{1}{4}$ teaspoon cayenne

Salt and pepper to taste

1 cup roasted corn kernels

2 15 ounce cans black beans rinsed and drained

½ cup fresh cilantro, chopped

Heat oil in a saucepan over medium heat; cook and stir onion and garlic until lightly browned, about 10 minutes.

Mix quinoa into onion mixture and cover with vegetable broth; season with cumin, cayenne pepper, salt, and pepper. Bring the mixture to a boil. Cover, reduce heat, and simmer until quinoa is tender and broth is absorbed, about 20 minutes.

Stir frozen corn into the saucepan, and continue to simmer until heated through, about 5 minutes; mix in the black beans and cilantro

Garlic Parmesan Red Potatoes

2 pounds red potatoes, cut into 4's
$\frac{1}{4}$ cup Extra virgin olive oil
4 cloves garlic, minced
1 teaspoon sea salt
1 teaspoon black pepper
2 tablespoons finely grated parmesan cheese
1 lemon juiced

Preheat oven to 350 degrees.

Place potatoes in an 8X8 inch baking dish.

In a small bowl combine extra virgin olive oil, garlic, salt and lemon juice; pour over potatoes and stir to coat.

Sprinkle parmesan cheese over potatoes.
Bake, covered, in a preheated oven for 30 minutes.

Uncover and bake until golden brown and tender when pierced with a fork, about 10 minutes more.

Roasted Vegetables

1 small butternut squash, cubed
2 red bell peppers, seeded and diced
3 Yukon potatoes, cubed
1 small red onion quartered
1 tablespoon chopped fresh thyme
2 tablespoons chopped fresh Rosemary
1/4 cup extra virgin olive oil
2 tablespoons balsamic vinegar
salt and black pepper to taste

Preheat oven to 475 degrees.

In a large bowl, combine the squash, red bell peppers
sweet potato, the Yukon Gold potatoes.

Separate the Red Onion quarters into pieces and add
them to the mixture.

In a small bowl, stir together thyme, Rosemary, olive oil
vinegar, salt, and pepper. Toss with vegetables until they
are coated. Spread evenly on a large roasting pan that is
lined with foil.

Roast for 35 to 40 minutes in a preheated oven, stirring
every 10 or 15 minutes until vegetables are cooked
through and browned.

SOUPS

Asian Ginger Noodle Soup (Serves 6)

This delicious soup can be made so many different ways.
You can add or subtract vegetables as you see fit.
Get creative and try variations of this.
Your family will love the versatility that this soup can
bring to your table.

2 tablespoons butter
1 teaspoon olive oil
6 cloves garlic, chopped
2 teaspoons ginger, chopped
1 tablespoon Tamari sauce
4 cups vegetable broth
2 cups of water
9 ounces Asian noodles
(rice noodles, or regular linguini will work as well)
$\frac{1}{2}$ cup green onions, chopped

-In a medium pot sauté garlic, ginger and butter in olive
oil for 2 minutes.
Add broth, water, and Tamari sauce
and bring to a boil and add noodles. Boil till al dente.

-Reduce heat and add green onions.

-Heat through.

Protein ideas:
You might want to add some protein to this delicious soup. Firm tofu, ground turkey, chicken or beef or you may want to add some healthy cooked sausage.

Experiment & Enjoy!

Beef and Pinto Bean Chili (Serves 6)

This simple chili can be a delicious dinner on a cold fall day! You can modify this recipe to use in a crock pot as well.

Extra virgin olive oil to coat pan
1 pound boneless chuck roast, trimmed and cut into 1-inch pieces
1/8 teaspoon salt
2 tablespoons extra virgin olive oil
1 large chopped onion
2 large minced jalapeño, peppers ribbed and seeded
10 garlic cloves, minced
1 12-ounce bottle or can of beer
1 tablespoon paprika
1 tablespoon ground cumin
2 tablespoons of ketchup
3 cups fat-free, lower-sodium beef broth
2 15 ounce cans of chopped tomatoes (no salt added)

-1 15-ounce can pinto beans, rinsed and drained
-Garnish...Avocado chunks, chopped cilantro leaves, sour cream, lime wedges.

-Heat a Dutch oven over high heat.

-Coat pan with extra virgin olive oil.

-Sprinkle beef evenly with salt.

-Add beef to pan; sauté 5 minutes, turning to brown on all sides.

-Remove from pan. Add oil to pan; swirl to coat. Add onion and jalapeño; sauté 8 minutes or until lightly browned, stirring occasionally.

-Add garlic; sauté 1 minute, stirring constantly.

-Stir in beer, scraping pan to loosen browned bits; bring to a boil. Cook until liquid almost evaporates (about 10 minutes), stirring occasionally.

-Stir in paprika, cumin, and tomato paste; cook 1 minute, stirring frequently.

-Add broth, tomatoes, beans and beef; bring to a boil. Reduce heat, and simmer 1 1/2 hours or until mixture is thick and beef is very tender, stirring occasionally.

-Ladle 1 cup chili into each of 6 bowls.

-Garnish with avocado chunks, chopped cilantro leaves, sour cream, lime wedges.

ENJOY!

Chicken and Corn Chowder (Serves 6)

A fall favorite, this chowder feels like "comfort food" in a bowl. Add a piece of crusty French bread for dipping and you have yourself an excellent meal.

2 tablespoons butter
1/2 cup chopped onion
1/2 cup chopped celery
1 jalapeño pepper, seeded, ribbed and minced
2 tablespoons all-purpose flour or Gluten Free Baking Flour
3 cups 2% reduced-fat milk or almond milk
2 cups chopped roasted skinless, boneless chicken
1 1/2 cups fresh or frozen corn kernels
1/4 teaspoon dried thyme
1/4 teaspoon ground pepper
1/8 teaspoon salt
1 (14 3/4-ounce) can cream-style corn

Melt the butter in a large Dutch oven over medium heat. Add onion, celery, and jalapeño; cook for 3 minutes or until tender, stirring frequently. Add flour; cook 1 minute, stirring constantly. Stir in milk and remaining ingredients. Bring to a boil; turn to low and simmer for about 15 minutes.

Hot and Sour Tofu Soup (Serves 6)

Are you feeling under the weather? This delicious soup is sure to heat things up in your body and speed the healing process. YUMMY!

1 package 14 ounces firm water-packed tofu, drained
1 $\frac{1}{2}$ cups water
1 package $\frac{1}{2}$ ounce dried sliced shiitake mushroom caps
4 cups fat-free, less-sodium chicken broth
$\frac{1}{4}$ cup white vinegar
2 tablespoons less-sodium soy sauce
2 tablespoon finely chopped peeled fresh ginger
2 teaspoons sugar
$\frac{3}{4}$ teaspoon pepper
2 garlic clove, minced
2 $\frac{1}{2}$ tablespoons cornstarch
$\frac{1}{4}$ cup warm water
$\frac{1}{2}$ cup canned sliced bamboo shoots, drained and cut into julienne strips
$\frac{1}{2}$ cup thinly diagonally sliced green onion tops

Place tofu on several layers of paper towels.
Cover tofu with several more layers of paper towels; top with a heavy cutting board to soak up all liquid.
Let stand 30 minutes.

Discard paper towels.

Cut tofu into 1-inch cubes.

Bring 1 1/2 cups water to a boil in a small saucepan; remove from heat.

Stir in mushrooms; let stand 30 minutes.

Stir in broth and next 6 ingredients. Bring to a boil. -- Reduce heat, and simmer 10 minutes, stirring occasionally.

Combine remaining 1/4 cup warm water and cornstarch in a small bowl, stirring with a whisk until smooth.

Stir cornstarch mixture, tofu, and bamboo shoots into broth mixture; bring to a boil.

Cook 5 minutes more and then ladle into bowls and top with green onion.

YUMMY!

Garden Minestrone with Pasta Shells

(Serves 6)

Classic... would be the best way to describe this simple but "family friendly" favorite. All of your vegetable goodness in one bowl.   What more could you ask for?

2 teaspoons extra virgin olive oil
1 cup chopped onion
2 teaspoons oregano, fresh, chopped
4 garlic cloves, minced
3 cups chopped yellow squash
3 cups chopped Mexican squash
1 cup chopped carrot
1 cup frozen corn kernels (thawed and rinsed)
1 can tomato sauce, 15 ounces
1 cup chopped tomato, divided
3 (14-ounce) cans fat-free, less-sodium chicken broth, divided (or homemade)
$\frac{1}{2}$ cup uncooked pasta shells or Gluten Free Shells
1 can Great Northern beans, rinsed and drained
1 10 ounce package frozen spinach rinsed and drained WELL
$\frac{3}{4}$ teaspoon salt

$\frac{1}{2}$ teaspoon freshly ground black pepper

Parmesan/ Romano blend shredded cheese for garnish

Heat oil in a large pot over medium-high heat.

Add onion to pan; sauté 3 minutes or until softened.

Add oregano and garlic; sauté 1 minute.

Stir in squash, carrot, and corn; sauté 5 minutes or until vegetables are tender. Remove from heat.

Add tomato sauce to pan; return pan to heat.

Stir in remaining 1 cup chopped tomato and remaining 2 cans broth; bring mixture to a boil.

Reduce heat, and simmer 20 minutes.

Add pasta and beans to pan; cook 10 minutes or until pasta is tender, stirring occasionally.

Remove from heat.

Stir in spinach, salt, and 1/2 teaspoon pepper.

Ladle soup into individual bowls; top with cheese.

Garnish with shredded cheese.

ENJOY!

Sauces, Salsas & Marinades

Thai Marinade

This marinade is used for chicken or pork

Ingredients:

1/4 cup low sodium soy sauce
3 tablespoons firmly packed dark brown sugar
2 tablespoons fresh lime juice
2 tablespoons extra virgin olive oil
1 tablespoon curry powder
3 garlic cloves, minced
1 teaspoon finely minced fresh ginger
1/2 teaspoon ground cardamom

Salsa Verde

Salsa verde is used as a condiment or dipping sauce for grilled meats, fish, poultry, or vegetables.

Ingredients:

2/3 cup lightly packed flat-leaf parsley leaves
3 tablespoons drained capers
2 garlic cloves
4 teaspoons fresh lemon juice
1/2 teaspoon Dijon mustard
1/2 teaspoon salt
1/4 teaspoon fresh-ground black pepper
1/4 cup olive oil
1/4 cup low sodium chicken broth

Preparation:

Put the parsley, capers, garlic, lemon juice, mustard, salt, and pepper into a food processor or blender.
Pulse just to chop, six to eight times.
With the machine running, add the oil and chicken broth in a thin stream to make a slightly coarse puree.
Just before serving, pulse to re-emulsify just before serving.

Sicilian Pesto

Ingredients:

- 2 cups lightly packed fresh basil leaves
- 1/2 cup fresh mint leaves
- 3 garlic cloves
- 1 to 2 serrano chilies, cored, and seeded, depending on how spicy you like your food
- 1 tablespoon hot red pepper flakes
- 1/2 teaspoon fennel seeds
- 1/4 cup sliced blanched almonds
- 1/2 cup extra virgin olive oil
- 1/4 cup plus $\frac{1}{4}$ cup freshly grated Pecorino Romano
- Salt

Preparation:

Place the basil, mint, garlic, chilies, red pepper flakes, fennel seeds, and almonds in a food processor and pulse three times to start the chopping process. Add in the oil in a thin stream and pulse four or five times to create a thick paste (not a thin, oily sauce). Add $\frac{1}{4}$ cup of the cheese and pulse once to mix it in.
Season the pesto with salt, if it needs it.

75

Homemade Italian Seasoning

(Makes about 2 cups)

- 1/2 cup dried basil
- 1/4 cup dried oregano
- 1/4 cup dried rosemary
- 1/4 cup dried marjoram
- 1/4 cup dried parsley
- 1/4 cup dried thyme
- 1/4 cup dried savory
- 2 tablespoon ground black pepper
- 1 1/2 tablespoons dried sage
- 1 teaspoon red pepper flakes

Combine all ingredients; store in an airtight glass container.

Chicken or Steak Italian Marinade

Ingredients:

- 1/3 cup olive oil

- 1/4 cup lemon juice

- 2 teaspoons oregano

- 2 tablespoons dry parsley

- 6 cloves garlic, crushed

- 1/4 teaspoon crushed red pepper flakes

Mix above ingredients. Use to marinate chicken or steak for up to 3 days in refrigerator.

Vegetable Marinade

Ingredients:

- 1 1/4 cups water
- 2 tablespoons balsamic vinegar
- 1/3 cup cider vinegar
- 2 tablespoons lemon juice
- 2 teaspoons white pepper
- 2 cloves garlic, minced
- 1/4 cups chopped parsley

Preparation:

Combine water, both vinegars, lemon juice, pepper, garlic and parsley in large saucepan.

Bring to a boil, cover, simmer 10 minutes.

Remove from heat.

Cool to room temperature, cover and chill at least 2-3 hours.

Drizzle over cooked vegetables.

Entrees

Chicken With Sofrito (Serves 4)

Cooking with wine brightens up my sense of smell.
It brings me back to the days of my Grandmas kitchen.
This delicious dish brings back fond memories!

1 tablespoon EVOO
8 pieces of boneless skinless chicken
(your choice of pieces)
Sea Salt and Pepper
1/2 cup Sofrito (recipe to follow)
1/3 cup dry white wine, such as Pinot Grigio
1/2 cup low sodium chicken broth
(I make my own, lower in sodium, better ingredients)

Preheat oven to 400 degrees
Heat oil in a large skillet. brown chicken quickly about 8
minutes and then flip chicken over and add Sofrito wine
and broth.
Combine the flavors and place all in a baking dish.
Bake in the oven for about 25 minutes or until meat
runs clear. Serve chicken pieces and spoon sauce over
the top.

Sofrito

2 pounds plum tomatoes, chopped
2 red bell peppers, seeded and chopped
2 medium yellow onions, chopped
6 cloves garlic, chopped
1 bunch cilantro, chopped

Pulse ALL in a blender or food processor until finely chopped, not pureed.
In a large pot heat 1/2 cup EVOO add mixture and cook for about 25 minutes till thickened and reduced

Serve this Chicken Sofrito with brown rice or with QUINOA and a garden salad to complete this meal.

Enjoy!!

Crock Pot Beef Stroganoff

Too busy to cook? This is a quick and easy meal that goes right in the crockpot... Turn it on and get to work. When you come home to the smell of this awesome meal, you'll have a huge smile on your face!!

Ingredients:
2 pounds stew meat, cubed
1 tablespoon cooking oil
1 cup mushrooms, sliced
1 tablespoon onion, minced
2 teaspoons garlic, minced
1 teaspoon oregano
1/2 teaspoon salt
1/2 teaspoon pepper
1/2 teaspoon thyme
1 bay leaf
2 cups beef broth
2/3 cup sherry
1 1/2 cups sour cream
1/2 cup flour
1/4 cup water
4 cups noodles, cooked

Preparation:

Brown beef in hot oil.

Drain fat.

Combine beef, mushrooms, onion, garlic, oregano, salt pepper, thyme, beef broth, sherry and bay leaf in slow cooker.

Cover; cook on High 4-5 hours.

Discard bay leaf.

Mix together sour cream, flour and water.

Stir one cup of the hot liquid into sour cream mixture.

Cover; cook on High for 30 minutes.

Serve over noodles.

SO GOOD!

Smothered Pork Chops and Kale

(Serves 4)

This delicious recipe is a keeper in our home.
I should have timed all of us eating.
This dish disappeared in minutes.
My family had no idea the vegetable was Kale till after their plates were cleaned.
Kale is well suited for this dish!

4 teaspoons of EVOO
4 pork sirloin chops (about the size of your palm or slightly bigger)
1 small onion chopped
2 cloves garlic chopped
1 $\frac{1}{2}$ cups of chicken or vegetable broth (I make homemade broth)
2 tablespoons of flour or gluten free flour
1 bunch of Kale leaves only, remove all stems and inside rib
Salt and pepper

-In a large skillet place EVOO and heat up.
Put lightly seasoned (with salt and pepper) pork chops in the skillet. Brown on both sides cooking thoroughly till almost done.

-Remove the pork chops to a platter and tent with foil to keep hot.

-Add onion and garlic to pan and sauté till brown.

-Add broth and flour.

Whisk to thicken to a gravy consistency.

-Add Kale and stir till wilted.

-Place chops back in the skillet moving them to the bottom of the pan and the kale wilted on top of the chops...use your judgment according to your stove on how high the heat should be... NOT too hot...

-At this point, place lid over skillet and turn down to low.

-Let steam a bit to make sure the pork is cooked and juices and blended.

-Serve with cooked Quinoa.

Broth for skillet and liquid for Quinoa as well......
When cooking Quinoa the recipe calls for 2 cups of water to 1 cup Quinoa. I use 2 cups of water and one bouillon cube to flavor the water.

For the recipe above I used one bouillon cube for the 1 ½ cups of water and didn't use as much salt on the chops.

ENJOY!

Quinoa Feta Burgers (Serves 6)

This recipe is dedicated to my friend Roni Hornstein.
Roni eats so healthy she makes me look bad!
I love Roni's wisdom about foods that are good for our
bodies!!   Life long friends are the best!

1 can (15 ounces) kidney beans, drained and rinsed
1 red onion, minced
1 carrot, finely grated
3 cups cooked quinoa
2 tablespoons chopped fresh parsley
3 tablespoons crumbled feta
2 eggs, lightly whisked
2 tablespoons extra-virgin olive oil
6 whole-wheat buns, grilled

-In a bowl, mash beans into a thick paste and mix in
onion, carrot, quinoa, parsley, feta, and eggs.
-Form mixture into six patties and chill 30 minutes.
-Heat 1 tablespoon oil in a skillet over medium-high
heat, directly on grill grates or on stove top, and cook
patties until golden (add remaining tablespoon oil if
cooking in batches), 4 to 5 minutes per side.
-Serve on buns with your choice of tomatoes, romaine
lettuce, onion slices, grilled onions, sautéed mushrooms
or even more cheese.

Spicy Shrimp With Lime & Cilantro

I have taken this recipe from Everyday Food May 2012 edition and made it my own by changing the ingredients to suit my family.

Serves 4. Total cooking time 15 minutes

$\frac{1}{4}$ teaspoon sea salt
1 teaspoon smoked paprika
$\frac{1}{2}$ teaspoon ground cumin
$\frac{1}{2}$ teaspoon ground curry
1/8 teaspoon cayenne pepper
1/8 teaspoons ground cinnamon
1 $\frac{1}{2}$ pound cooked shrimp peeled and deveined (not frozen)
1 1/2 tablespoon butter
-Chopped cilantro and lime wedges

-Start your water to boil to cook either whole wheat pasta or quinoa. This will probably take a bit longer than the shrimp so get this cooking.

-Combine dry ingredients in a bowl. Salt, paprika, cumin, curry, cayenne pepper and cinnamon and blend well. Toss in shrimp and gently stir to coat shrimp evenly.

-In a large skillet add butter and shrimp simmer to heat through and blend flavors. It will probably take 10 minutes.

-Serve the shrimp over quinoa or whole wheat pasta. And sprinkle cilantro and lime. If you wish you can also add the lime to the skillet the last 1 minute of cooking to blend flavors.

-Other topping can include pine nuts, slivered almonds, golden raisins or maybe even pumpkin seeds.

ENJOY!

Ultimate Bolognese Sauce and Spaghetti Squash

Ingredients

1 pound of ground beef
½ pound turkey bacon, chopped
2 medium carrots, chopped
1 small yellow onion, chopped
4 cloves minced garlic
2 medium tomatoes, chopped
1 can tomato paste
¾ cup coconut milk
½ cup beef stock
2 teaspoons dried oregano
1 teaspoon sea salt
1 teaspoon black pepper
1 small to medium spaghetti squash cut in half and seeded.

Preparation
In a large skillet, Sauté carrots, onions, garlic and tomatoes.
Add ground beef and cook all the way through on low.
Stir in
Tomato paste, milk, broth, oregano, sea salt and black pepper.
Simmer on low for 30 minutes stirring occasionally.

Black Bean and Cheese Enchiladas with Ranchero Sauce

Ingredients

2 dried ancho chilies, stemmed and seeded
2 cups water
2 teaspoons olive oil
1 cup chopped yellow onion
5 garlic cloves, sliced
2 cups organic low-sodium vegetable broth
2 tablespoons chopped fresh oregano
2 tablespoons no-salt-added tomato paste
1/2 teaspoon ground cumin
1 tablespoon fresh lime juice
1/8 teaspoon ground red pepper
1 (15-ounce) can black beans, rinsed and drained
2 cups (8 ounces) shredded 4-cheese Mexican-blend cheese, divided
3 thinly sliced green onions, divided
Cooking spray
12 (6-inch) corn tortillas
6 tablespoons sour cream

Preparation

1. Preheat oven to 400°.
2. Combine chilies and 2 cups water in a saucepan; bring to a boil, reduce heat, and simmer 5 minutes.
3. Remove from heat; let stand 5 minutes.
4. Drain

Chicken Meatballs and Chimichurri Sauce

Meatballs

1 1/2 lb. ground chicken;

1 egg, eaten;

2 green onions, minced;

3 garlic cloves, minced;

2 tsp. dried parsley

Coconut oil;

Sea salt and freshly ground black pepper to taste

Sauce

1/2 cup fresh parsley, minced;

3/4 cup extra virgin olive oil;

1/4 cup red wine vinegar;

4 to 5 garlic cloves, minced;

2 green onions, sliced;

2 tbsp. fresh oregano, minced;

1/2 tsp. red pepper flakes;

1 tbsp. fresh lemon juice;

Sea salt and freshly ground black pepper;

Preparation

Mix all of meatball ingredients. (Do not over mix or meat will come out tough).

Using wet hands, roll meatballs.

On a foil lined cookie sheet, bake meatballs at 375 degrees for 25 minutes.

Meanwhile, mix all ingredients for sauce.

YUMMY!!

A Final Heart Felt Message From Sharon

In the 24 years I have been studying nutrition and raising my family, I have had numerous mentors to help me along the way. They have come from all walks of life, each with their own perspective and experience, there to guide and support me.

My children, Alan and Melissa have been my biggest fans. They've always believed in their mom and I will always believe in them.

For everyone that has been a part of my journey, I am eternally grateful.

I believe the message that eating "Real" food leads to living a happier, healthy life has never been more timely. I am always looking for new ways to provide people with this message of empowerment.

I hope you will join me on my Journey to help you "make sense of food"!

Sharon

Media and Events

You can get more info on my upcoming weekend health and wellness retreats (Health Haven) and to my NEW Health & Wellness Royal Caribbean cruises, at my Website: **www.foodsenseatoz.com**

Join the conversation with other foodies on my Facebook page at
https://www.facebook.com/FoodsenseAtoZ

On Twitter
https:/twitter.com/FoodSenseAtoZ

On Instagram
https://www.instagram.com/sharonmadsen/

On Linkedin
https://www.linkedin.com/in/foodsenseatoz/

My Blog:
https://medium.com/@sharonmadsen

A word of Thanks to those that made this work possible.

Dan Watts

Dan is a good friend, an architect in a past life, and my media genius. We have worked on three different web sites with online e-commerce, helped promote my radio show, designed print marketing, created promotional videos for my Health & Wellness cruise and weekend retreat series and designed my recent book cover... all with a camera in his hand.
Our brainstorming meetings are so much fun because anything is possible with him.

If you ever get the chance to work with Dan Watts on any media/marketing project, he won't disappoint. His "out of the box" thinking is incredible! Thanks Dan.
www.nextworldmedia.com

Steve Hoover
Editor and Event Producer
Steve's patience and persistence as an editor has been huge. We have come a long way and are still friends. He always has the right way to say it!

Steve also knows how to manage a successful event. If you want an event to run like a watch call Steve.
stevehoover@cox.
602-284-9931

53918132R00060

Made in the USA
San Bernardino, CA
03 October 2017